30151000232236

This book may be kept
FOURTEEN DAYS
A fine will be charged for each
day the book is kept overtime.

D1788873

AUG. 1 1981		
AUG. 25 1981		
AUG. 28 1981		

```
428.1
Te      Tester, Sylvia Root
            Opposite Odeila.  By Sylvia Root Tester.
        A book of Antonyms.  Illustrated by John Keely.
        Elgin, Il.  Childrens Press.  c.1978.
            31p.   illus.


            1.English language-synonyms and antonyms.
        I.Keely, John, Illus.  II.Title.
```

COLOMA PUBLIC LIBRARY

Opposite Odelia

A Book of Antonyms

Words that mean the opposite.

by Sylvia Root Tester
illustrated by John Keely

THE CHILD'S WORLD

ELGIN, ILLINOIS 60120

Distributed by Childrens Press, 1224 West Van Buren Street, Chicago, Illinois 60607.

Library of Congress Cataloging in Publication Data

Tester, Sylvia Root, 1939-
  Opposite Odelia: a book of Antonyms, words that mean the opposite.

  SUMMARY: An easy-to-read introduction to antonyms, words with opposite meanings.
  1. English language—Synonyms and antonyms—Juvenile literature. [1. English language—Synonyms and antonyms] I. Keely, John. II. Title.
PE1591.T44   428'.1   78-5294
ISBN 0-89565-036-3

© 1978 The Child's World, Inc.
All rights reserved. Printed in U.S.A.

dangerous – safe

fall

rise

angry

dry

bad

clean – dirty

kind – mean

fast – slow

wild – tame

same – different

push – pull

give – take

careless – careful

noisy – quiet

clumsy – graceful

bold – shy

hateful

loving